A message from

The EARL of STRATHMORE and KINGHORNE

My family have lived at Glamis Castle since 1372 when Sir John Lyon was granted the thaneage of Glamis by King Robert II. In 1376 Sir John married the King's daughter, Princess Joanna. Since then Glamis has been visited and lived in by many members of the Scottish and British Royal Families. The Castle has been added to and altered throughout the centuries and it continues to evolve even now. I am pleased to welcome you and I trust that the glimpse you will see of what has passed will prove interesting, but it should be remembered that it is still a home to which I and my family are extremely attached. I hope to maintain the Castle in as good a condition or better than you see it now. I hope you will enjoy your visit. It would afford me great pleasure should you wish to come again with your friends.

Strathmore and Kinghorne

Contents

A trophy of swords, axes, pistols and pieces of armour to be seen in the Crypt

Approach to the Castle

Daniel Defoe, writing in the early 18th century, expressed wonder at Glamis's many spires, turrets, towers and statues and likened the place to a city.

The modern visitor seeing the Castle for the first time at the end of its long avenue cannot but draw breath in admiration as did Defoe. Entrance is through the *'De'll Gates'* in the park wall, adorned with heraldic beasts and satyrs. This once stood in front of the Castle and was set up there in 1680 by a local mason, Alexander Crow, to Lord Strathmore's design. After a short distance the driveway turns into a grand tree-lined avenue leading to the Castle. To the left is a *'doo'cot'* (dovecote). On the right is a tree which can be seen from the Castle and was the point where courting domestics had to stop so that they could be *'chaperoned'* by watchful eyes from the Castle's windows.

In the late 17th century there were outer defences of walls and towers enclosing formal parterres. These were swept away in 1772-75 with the intention of remodelling the park in the fashion of Lancelot 'Capability' Brown. Finally completed in the mid-19th century, the park now resembles the surroundings of an English Palladian mansion and contrasts strongly with the rugged, ancient and mysterious building which dominates it. These changes infuriated Sir Walter Scott when he came here and outraged his sense of history. All that is left of these outer defences and decorations are the sundial and the statues of James VI and his son Charles I.

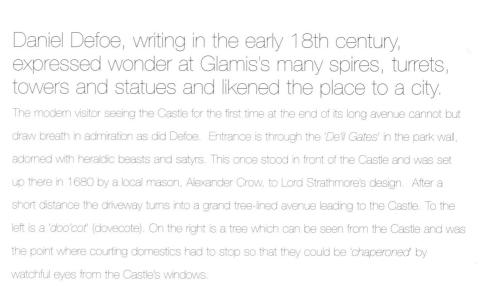

Although visitors to the Castle enter through a door on the north side, the main entrance to the building faces the drive in the angle tower which was begun shortly after 1600 by the 1st Earl of Kinghorne. This work was completed by the 3rd Earl and his bust can be seen above the door in a circular niche above the Royal Arms.

Top: the Castle seen from the avenue, and below, the 'doo' cot' (dovecote) and underneath an heraldic beast above the 'De'll Gates' & the baroque sundial. Lions stand guard at the Castle entrance

Right: King James VI & I; one of Arnold Quellin's 17th century lead statues on the Castle lawn

Dining Room

The silver nef, or ship centrepiece, was presented to the 13th Earl and his Countess by estate tenants to celebrate the couple's golden wedding in 1903

The entire wing in which this room is situated was demolished in 1775 and rebuilt in 1798 -1801.

The Dining Room was designed later by the Hon. Thomas Liddell, great-grandson of the 8th Earl of Strathmore, in 1851-53. The centrepiece of the room is the elaborate fireplace with its massive oak armorial overmantel bearing the carved arms of the 12th Earl of Strathmore. The table is laid with silver, china, cutlery and glass used by the 13th and 14th Earls.

In the sideboard alcove are two full-length portraits of the 13th Earl and his wife Frances Dora, née Smith. To the right is another full-length portrait of Charlotte Grinstead, widow of Lord Glamis (son of the 11th Earl), and mother of the 12th and 13th Earls. To the left of the fireplace is Patrick Lord Glamis, the Queen Mother's eldest brother who became 15th Earl in 1944. He is in the uniform of a Lieutenant in the Scots Guards. Among the other family portraits in this room are those of the present Earl and Countess of Strathmore by Andrew Festing, and a charming conversation piece showing the Drawing Room with the 14th Earl and Countess (the parents of Her Majesty Queen Elizabeth the Queen Mother). The history of the family is told in this room by means of heraldry. All round the walls are wooden shields showing the family alliances and the stained glass shows the evolution of the Strathmore arms which were changed again in 1937.

In days gone by, terrified servants would need to check when the next course was required... a spyhole in the room's painted Dutch screen, provided the necessary concealment !

IN COMMEMORATION OF THE GOLDEN WEDDING OF CLAUD & FRANCES, EARL & COUNTESS OF STRATHMORE AND KINGHORN MICHAELMAS DAY 1903. THIS CLOCK IS PRESENTED BY THEIR LOVING GRANDCHILDREN.

MARY	MURIEL				
PATRICK	CHARLES				
JOHN	GEOFFREY	HUBERT			
ALEXANDER	DORIS	JOAN	GAVIN	PHYLLIS	ALFRED
FERGUS	WINIFRED	EFFIE	ANGUS	LESLIE	ALEX
ROSE	RONALD	ERNESTINE	LYON	HILDA	JESSUP
MICHAEL	LILIAN	LYON		BLACKBURN	
ELIZABETH	LYON				
DAVID					
LYON					

The Glamis lion (above left), was a Golden Wedding present to the 13th Earl and Countess from their children, and there is a grandfather clock given to them by their grandchildren on the same occasion. The engraved plaque (left), is hidden within the clock door. The Dining table is dressed with other decorative items based on the lion motif

The Dining room ceiling is adorned by the thistles of Scotland, roses of England and lions of the Lyon family

The 16th century 'kitchen' was formed out of two of three barrel-vaulted cellars. It may have originally been intended as a lower hall or guardroom. It was restored in 1990 and is used for private receptions.

Crypt

Walking through the door leading from the Dining Room to the Crypt, is to pass in a few seconds from the era of Queen Victoria to the Middle Ages.

This so-called Crypt was the Lower Hall of the 15th century tower house, where the lord's retainers would dine. The present wide stair from the front door is a 19th century alteration to an existing staircase in the same position built by the 1st Earl of Kinghorne. The width of the Crypt walls can be judged by looking at the windows. There are many objects of interest to be seen. Chain mail hanging here dates from the 19th century. There are numerous big game heads and trophies of arms and armour and even a saddle, a relic of Cromwell's occupation together with Jacobean oak furniture. This is one of the oldest, strongest and most impregnable parts of the building.

The old well at the bottom of the stair was the Castle's only source of water, but has long since dried up. Many years ago silver plate and other valuables were discovered hidden in it.

The secret chamber, about which are woven many legends, is thought to be located deep in the thickness of the Crypt walls on the left as you face the two small windows at the end. In this room it is said that one of the Lords of Glamis and the 'Tiger' Earl of Crawford played cards with the Devil himself on the Sabbath. So great were the resulting disturbances that eventually the room was built up and permanently sealed 300 years later.

The 3rd Earl of Strathmore and Kinghorne surrounded by his sons, left to right: John (later 4th Earl), Charles and Patrick Lyon of Auchterhouse M.P., by Jacob de Wet 1683

Wearing a fabulous Romanesque tunic, with 'lion' epaulettes, he gestures towards Glamis, the castle he restored and remodelled, and which remains very much the same today

Drawing Room

The Rev. John Stirton, in his book on Glamis writes of the Drawing Room, formerly Earl Patrick's 'Great Hall' thus: *'The most splendid apartment in the Castle.* It is sixty feet long by twenty two feet broad and has a fine arched ceiling of beautiful old plasterwork, bearing the monograms of John, second Earl of Kinghorne and his Countess, Margaret Erskine, daughter of the Earl of Mar, and the date, 1621. The 3rd Earl had a great liking for this room and speaks of it in his "Book of Record" as "my great hall which is a room that I have ever loved". Three great windows, deeply embrasured in the walls, which here are eight feet in thickness, give light to the room.' A chamber at one end of the room formed out of the thickness of the walls is called the Powder Room.

The 14th Earl and his Countess in the Drawing Room. They were the parents of HM Queen Elizabeth the Queen Mother

From top: Lady Elizabeth Lyon, Countess of Aboyne; John Grahame of Claverhouse, Viscount Dundee by Kneller; Queen Elizabeth I; King Charles I after Van Dyck

The bleak stones which must have characterised its original appearance were plastered and the 2nd Earl continued the process by employing several stuccoists working in the Italian style to embellish the ceiling and to create a frieze. Thus the room evolved from primitive Great Hall to elegant Drawing Room. The plaster overmantel with its caryatids and royal arms was probably completed a few years earlier. The white plaster has been picked out in colour and now shows the royal arms in all the glory of its heraldic colours surrounded by a green thistle and rose motif and this is as it should be. The pink wash on the walls makes a

The 3rd Earl's jewel cabinet

19th century porcelain figurines stand either side of a French clock decorated with ormolu

perfect background for the family portraits which abound in this room, notably the enormous conversation piece of the 3rd Earl with his sons and hunting dogs. This picture is particularly interesting as it shows the Castle as reconstructed by the Earl almost to its present appearance and some of the outer gates and walls which have disappeared can be distinguished.

Right: a detail of the painting of Lady Arabella Stuart

Below: large carved and gilded lions stand guard either side of the fireplace

Another notable portrait is that of the young 9th Lord Glamis (afterwards 1st Earl of Kinghorne) aged eight by an unknown artist of the school of Clouet backed with a portrait of his secretary George Boswell. Beneath the large conversation piece are portraits of Lady Arabella Stuart, King Charles I and Queen Elizabeth I. Especially interesting is the fine portrait of John Grahame of Claverhouse, Viscount Dundee, known as *'Bonnie Dundee'*. One of Scotland's most dashing heroes, he supported King James VII and II at the Revolution of 1688 and raised an army in the Highlands with the help of Cameron of Lochiel. At a fierce battle in the perilous Pass of Killiecrankie he defeated William III's General Mackay, but in the moment of victory fell mortally wounded. According to Michael Barrington this portrait, by Kneller, inspired Scott, who saw it on his visit here, to describe it in *'Redgauntlet'*. Dundee's seat was at Claverhouse Castle. Nothing remains of it above ground but the site near Glenogilvy is known and is now part of the Glamis estate.

Chapel

It was in this very chapel that James VIII (*The Old Chevalier*) touched local people for the *'King's Evil'* or scrofula. Although not a *de facto* sovereign he was *de jure* King of Scots and therefore his success in curing those who came from far and wide was not considered unusual.

The richly decorated panels on walls and ceiling make this one of the most beautiful small private chapels in Europe. It occupies one floor of a small wing added to the north east corner of the Castle from 1679 - 1683 by the 3rd Earl of Strathmore. The paintings were added in 1688 when the Earl commissioned Jacob de Wet; a Dutch artist brought to Scotland in 1673, to work on commissions for the Palace of Holyroodhouse in Edinburgh. The contract, dated 18 January 1688, stated that de Wet was to receive £90 and the paintings were to conform to scenes in Lord Strathmore's bible. That Bible has not been traced but recent research suggests that the ceiling panels were based on engravings by Boetius a Bolswert, dated 1622, and the wall paintings on engravings by Jacquet Callot published in 1631. One of the curiosities of these scenes is that depicting *Christ mistaken for a gardener and wearing a hat*. Other scenes show *The Last Supper, The Flight into Egypt, St. Andrew* and other Saints.

Christ depicted wearing a hat

The Chapel fell into disuse for some years but in 1866 it was restored by the 13th Earl and dedicated to St. Michael and All Angels. The stained glass window showing St. Michael was inserted in 1867-68 and the windows in the north wall, made by Kempe of London, were added in 1882-83. In 1979-80 the paintings were cleaned and restored by the *Stenhouse Conservation Centre* in Edinburgh. On the Feast Day of St. Michael in 1988 a service was held here for the Chapel's tercentenary and HM Queen Elizabeth the Queen Mother unveiled a plaque to commemorate the occasion. The Strathmore family regularly use the chapel today.

St. Andrew, Scotland's patron saint

The Last Supper

A detail from the large painting in the room;
'The Fruit Market' by Frans Snyders

A pair of 17th century panels needleworked by a
young girl: top - The return of Jacob and
below - The sacrifice of Isaac

Giltwood and tapestry
firescreen incorporating
the family crest and
the Arms of the
Bowes Lyons'

Billiard Room

This room, built between 1773 and 1776, is situated immediately above the great kitchen and houses what is left of the extensive library once at Glamis and which was dispersed a long time ago. Nevertheless some interesting volumes remain.

The plaster ceiling with its monograms and coronet reminiscent of the ceiling in King Malcolm's Room (the next room to be seen) does not date from the 17th century but was made for the 13th Earl in 1903 to commemorate his Golden Wedding. The huge fireplace which so well befits this room was brought here from Gibside, one of the seats of the Bowes family in County Durham. It bears the coats of arms of the Blakistons of Gibside, whose heiress Elizabeth, daughter of Sir Francis Blakiston, 3rd and last baronet, married Sir William Bowes of Streatlam Castle. The 9th Earl married Sir William's granddaughter, Mary Eleanor, heiress to extensive property in the North of England which strengthened the Lyon family's ties in that area.

This light, beautifully proportioned room has no feeling of menace and only emanates friendliness. Prominent above the large 19th century serving table is 'The Fruit Market' - a huge painting attributed to the great Flemish animal and still-life painter Frans Snyders. On either side hang the colours of the 1st Battalion The Black Watch, laid up in 1998.

The tapestries depicting *scenes from the life of King Nebuchadnezzar* are very rare, the only other known sets being at Knole in Kent and at Powys Castle in Wales. They were made about 1680 in England and are attributed to Thomas Poyntz. Above the fireplace hang the colours of the 2nd Battalion The Scots Guards, laid up in 1988, and a Bowes Lyon banner.

The pair of 17th century needlework panels depicting *Abraham and Isaac*, and *Jacob cheating Esau of his birthright* are thought to have been worked by young ladies of the family. The portraits include the father of Mary Eleanor, Sir George Bowes, and her son the 10th Earl of Strathmore by Mather Brown (see page 43).

King Malcolm's Room

This is not the actual room in which King Malcolm II died in 1034, but it may be near the site of the original chamber of the hunting lodge.

Pieces from the three armorial services made for the family in the 18th century; hand-painted porcelain of the Ch'ien Lung period

The glory of this room is its plasterwork, especially in the ceiling which bears the monograms of the 2nd Earl of Kinghorne and his first wife Lady Margaret Erskine together with medallion heads of Roman characters such as *Tarquin and Lucretia*. The arms of the 2nd Earl above the fireplace, as with the royal arms in the Drawing Room, have been picked out in full heraldic colours and add a new dimension to the room. The carved wooden chimneypiece is something of a *trompe l'oeil* since it is partly made from embossed and highly polished leather.

The wall hangings with *petit point* designs were worked in the 17th century by the wife of the 3rd Earl of Strathmore, Lady Helen Middleton, and were originally used as bed hangings for a four-poster bed. Looking closely you can see birds, animals and fruit worked straight into the linen. The china is part of the three armorial services made for the family in the 18th century and is hand-painted porcelain of the Ch'ien Lung period (1736-95). Its decoration is principally heraldic and shows the tressured blue lion on its own (for Lyon), the three bows (for Bowes) and the Bowes shield surmounting the Lyon lion, for the 9th Earl who married the Bowes heiress. In 1947 part of the service was given by the 15th Earl to his niece, HRH The Princess Elizabeth, as a wedding present when she married HRH Prince Philip. Her Majesty The Queen kindly returned it to Glamis to be restored to the rest of the service.

Following Lady Elizabeth Bowes Lyon's marriage into the Royal Family in 1923, her mother, the Countess of Strathmore, was later to arrange the following three rooms, previously used as bedrooms, to serve as a private suite whenever the royal couple visited Glamis.

HM Queen Elizabeth the Queen Mother when Duchess of York. Copy of a portrait by de Laszlo and right: The Arms of HM Queen Elizabeth the Queen Mother

The Queen Mother's Sitting Room

French night-light clock

The carved oak chimneypiece in this room with its matching overmantel, makes a suitable place to display the collection of Dutch and Chinese porcelain. The piece of tapestry set into the overmantel is from the cut-down tapestry in the Billiard Room. The ancient oak press with its elaborate carvings is worthy of note as are the tapestries which Lady Strathmore restored to their rightful place after they had been stored away for years. There is a small stone seat just inside the door and a little ghostly figure of a boy servant has been seen sitting there patiently waiting...... In the corridor, before entering the Queen Mother's Bedroom, there are several family portraits including *John, 4th Earl of Strathmore.*

The Queen Mother's Bedroom

In this room is a copy of the beautiful portrait of HM Queen Elizabeth The Queen Mother when Duchess of York, by de Laszlo (opposite). Other portraits here are of Her Majesty's brothers and sisters. The four-poster with its tall fluted columns and carved gilt fretwork top with its hangings has been restored.

On the four-poster bed the padded headboard has a scroll design with thistles and the bed-hangings, worked by Lady Strathmore, are of particular interest; inside the bed's pelmet is embroidered the monogram 'C & C' for Claude and Cecilia (the 14th Earl and Countess) and the names of all their children and their dates of birth, including 'Elizabeth 1900' and 'Michael 1893' grandfather of the present Earl.

The Queen Mother's Bedroom in the Dolls' House

The Dining Room in the Dolls' House

Embroidered and presented by the Countess of Strathmore to her husband, the 14th Earl on the occasion of their golden wedding in 1931

The King's Room

This was King George VI's Dressing Room and contains the recently restored Kinghorne Bed. It has three outer valances with central panels of applied silk decorated with straight stitches and couching. They are from a bed made for the 3rd Earl of Kinghorne in the late 17th century and bear his coat of arms.

John 4th Earl of Strathmore

Below: James IV and his granddaughter
Mary Queen of Scots

Spy-hole looking out to
the front entrance of the Castle

Duncan's Hall

Among the oldest and eeriest parts of the Castle, Duncan's Hall, like King Malcolm's Room, commemorates an historical event - the slaying of King Duncan by Macbeth. Although the killing took place near Elgin, this is the traditional scene of the crime. The portraits are those of King James IV and his grand-daughter, Mary Queen of Scots. The Queen visited Glamis on 22nd August 1562. The Shakespeare connection can probably be explained by the following chain of circumstances. The play *Macbeth* was written for James VI and I after his accession to the throne of England, bringing with him Scottish courtiers and Scottish customs. While King of Scots only, James had befriended the 9th Lord Glamis and often visited Glamis Castle. When Lord Glamis married the daughter of Lord Tullibardine, the King allowed the ceremony to take place in the Palace of Linlithgow. In 1603 Lord Glamis accompanied his royal master to England and three years later the King elevated him to the earldom of Kinghorne. The Earl died in 1615. It is possible that Shakespeare heard stories of Glamis which he used as a fit setting for the grim tragedy of *Macbeth*.

The Family Exhibition

Silver watch which belonged to the
Old Pretender, James VIII and III
(see the history of the 5th Earl
on page 42)

Exhibition Rooms

In order to display some of the exceptionally
interesting articles which have accumulated at
Glamis over the centuries, the Blue Room has
been adapted into a small museum known as
'The Family Exhibition'.

Here can be seen James VIII's watch and presentation sword, Claverhouse's leather

bullet-proof jerkin, Victorian dolls, the 14th Earl's uniforms, the robes worn at the

Coronation of Edward VII in 1902 and at subsequent coronations, and many other

fascinating objects.

Another exhibition is contained in the Coach House beneath the Dining Room. It

includes additional information on the Strathmore family, the construction of the Castle

and the development of the policies and gardens. A large part is also devoted to today's

management of the Estate.

Bullet-proof leather jerkin
which once belonged to
the charismatic and
dashing 'Bonnie Dundee',
John Grahame of
Claverhouse

18th century
uniform of the
Royal Company
of Archers
(The Queen's Bodyguard
in Scotland)

The Coach House
Museum

One of a pair of silver
gilt nutcrackers adorned
with the family lion

Silver box containing
the freedom of the
Burgh of Forfar
presented to
the 14th Earl in 1923

Castle Facilities

The Castle facilities include four shops, selling a wide range of quality gifts, souvenirs, books, antiques, paintings by local artists, knitwear, plants, clothing, Scottish produce and a restaurant which caters for up to 96 people.

Cricket Pavilion Shops

Recently restored and moved to its present position by the Castle, the Pavilion was originally built in 1890 by the 13th Earl and located by the cricket pitch in the south west corner of the Park. The Pavilion houses a small cricketing exhibition.

Kitchen Shop

Restaurant

The Restaurant is situated in the magnificent old Castle Kitchens with their 19th century ovens, stoves and copper pans carefully preserved.
The self-service, licensed, restaurant serves morning coffees, light lunches and afternoon teas.

Corporate Entertaining

illuminated by night

A formal dinner in the State Dining Room

Fireworks display in the grounds

© Brian Cowan Photolab - Forfar

16th century Kitchens

Glamis Castle is suitable for private receptions, lunch parties, grand dinners, cocktail parties, fashion shows, product launches, musical evenings, filming and wedding receptions. The State Apartments are available outside normal opening hours and the 16th Century Kitchens throughout the day. Dinner parties are held in the State Dining Room with drinks in the Great Drawing Room. Ideal numbers are 36 but up to 90 can be seated. Private lunch parties are held in the 16th Century Kitchens where up to 40 can be seated.

The Park is suitable for many outdoor events such as craft fairs, archery competitions, clay pigeon shooting, activity days, shows, rallies, musical evenings, equestrian events and filming.

The Jester's motley (see page 41)

27

Gardens & Policies

Introduction

There is evidence of planting and landscaping at Glamis stretching back some five centuries. At one time the Castle was surrounded by extensive walled gardens, created by the 3rd Earl in the late 17th century and seen in Jacob de Wet's portrait of him which hangs in the Castle. These were swept away by the 9th Earl at the end of the 18th century and replaced by an extensive landscape park. Much of the planting which provides the setting for the Castle today, including many fine conifers, was done by the 13th Earl after 1865.

The Forecourt and Dutch Garden

18th century maps and pictures show this area as an enclosed courtyard flanked by two rectangular walled gardens, the corners of which were marked by the two circular turrets which stand on the lawns in front of the Castle. The only parts of these old gardens which survive are the 17th century sundial, the two statues which stand at the foot of the Avenue, and two old yew trees which stood in what was once known as the *'flower garden'*. The garden walls were taken down in the 1770s. The small sunken garden on one side of the forecourt, known as the Dutch Garden, was created in 1893 to designs by Arthur Castings of London. It is laid out in a formal way with flower beds bounded by low box hedges, and with a small statue of *Mercury, messenger of the gods*, as its focal point. The garden is private but can be easily viewed from the Castle forecourt.

The Avenue

The mile-long avenue by which you arrive at the Castle was first planted by Earl Patrick in the 17th century. Although it was removed by the 9th Earl before the end of the 18th century, it was reinstated again by about 1850. At one time the approach to the Castle was made through a series of grand ornamental gateways set at intervals along the avenue – as seen in the 3rd Earl's portrait. These gateways were removed in 1775 and rebuilt around the edge of the policies. A second great avenue crossed the main approach to the Castle at right angles. Several old lime trees in the car park, and a few old trees at the foot of the sunken wall or *ha-ha* which separates the gardens from the policies, are all that remain of the 3rd Earl's planting.

The Italian Garden and Nature Trail

The Italian Garden in the wood to the east of the Castle was laid out by Lady Cecilia, wife of the 14th Earl, *c*.1910 to designs by Arthur Castings. Bounded by yew hedges, this garden includes a raised terrace between two small gazebos, from which one can look down on a fan-shaped parterre of formal beds separated by gravel walks. Other features include pleached alleys of beech, a stone fountain and ornamental gates which commemorate the Queen Mother's 80th birthday. Near the entrance to the Italian Garden is the start of a Nature Trail some three-quarters of a mile in length. Here the keen observer will be able to spot most of the flora and fauna which characterise the Glamis policies.

The Pinetum and Walled Garden

Walks lead you eastwards from the Castle across the Glamis Burn to the Pinetum, an area planted by the 13th Earl *c*.1870 with a variety of exotic trees, many of them conifers from North America. Following a period of neglect which began with the death of the 14th Earl in 1944, the 18th Earl has recently restored and begun to replant and redevelop this area. Along the northern edge of the Pinetum lies the Water of Dean, a small burn which drains the Loch of Forfar, and which runs onwards to join the River Tay. This was canalised in the 18th century to improve the drainage from the surrounding farmland. The burn is crossed by the Earl Michael Bridge, originally built in 1890, and reopened by HM The Queen Mother in 1996 after restoration by the 18th Earl. The four acre brick-walled kitchen garden is approached by a grass ramp leading through what were once terraced flower gardens. The walled garden was built for the 13th Earl between 1866 and 1868 to designs by Archibald Fowler of Castle Kennedy, at a cost of £7,500. It has been kept under grass for some years. There is a small exhibition to be found in the garden.

The baroque sundial   Earl John's Bridge built in 1697   Formal topiary is a striking feature of the Italian Garden

The pets' cemetery

Lions guard the entrance to the Dutch Garden

A pleached alley of beech seen through an arch in the Italian Garden

The boy and the dolphin fountain in the Italian Garden   Wrought iron gates at the entrance to the Walled Garden   © B. Cowan

The Estate

The much-admired Highland Cattle

Estate shepherds with their flock

Pig farming

Felling larch, the mainstay of the Estate's forestry

Glamis Castle is more than a family home and historic residence. Glamis Castle and Glamis Village are the focus of a traditional rural estate which today supports and encourages the development of a thriving rural community.

The Estate has developed over many centuries and today comprises a wide variety of properties and business and leisure activities. The policy has always been to maintain and restore the traditional parts of the Estate, whilst at the same time supporting and encouraging the rural community to ensure as many people as possible are able to have jobs and live in the countryside.

The Estate employs a Farms Director who supervises seven farms totalling 4500 acres. There are pigs, sheep, commercial cattle and highland cattle, the last of which are always admired by visitors to the Castle. The arable operation grows wheat, barley, oilseed rape and vegetables including cauliflower, broccoli, carrots and potatoes. Once again, although the most modern tractors and machinery are used to produce the food, great care is taken to enhance and conserve the wildlife habitats in hedgerows and field margins which are so important in today's modern agriculture.

Much of the village of Glamis was built by the Earl of Strathmore around 1760 and the policy with all dwellings is to maintain the character of these buildings whilst providing modern accommodation for those living in the rural community. The woods on the Estate have remained in continuous forestry for many centuries, and on a plan dated 1788, have almost identical boundaries to the present day. There is thus a wide range of tree species with some large and very spectacular ancient trees. On a rural estate all the various activities influence and affect each other and the best example of this is the wildlife and sporting shooting. The pheasant shooting employs several gamekeepers and part-time staff and attracts visiting guests from the rest of Britain and abroad. The income from this allows funds to be available which benefit all other forms of wildlife by enabling us to retain rough areas which are not planted with commercial trees and areas of crop planted especially for some birds rather than being sown with a crop of barley. When areas of forestry are being replanted open areas can be left and a proportion of hardwood trees planted to diversify the forest for the benefit of wildlife. Like any other estate, Strathmore Estates encourages a diversity of businesses in order to provide employment in the rural area.

The Estate is fortunate however to have a large tourism operation centred on the Castle which brings in many tens of thousands of visitors each year and in so doing, supports many jobs throughout the County of Angus in local hotels, bed and breakfasts, restaurants and other businesses. As well as the formal gardens and grounds of the Castle public access is encouraged on other parts of the Estate through woodland areas where locals and visitors alike can relax, exercise dogs and enjoy the wildlife which surrounds them. If the Estate can survive it will continue to benefit and encourage a great number of people, both employed and those completely outside the Estate, who wish to live and work in a thriving rural community.

The Village

*St. Fergus Church and the Pictish standing
stone c. 9th-10th century*

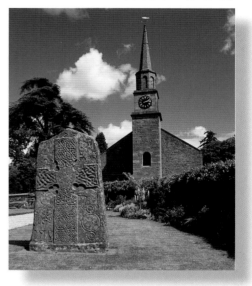

Evidence of man's habitation around Glamis can be traced back to the Picts.

From the 4th-9th century A.D., they controlled virtually all of Scotland. The carved standing stone in the manse garden, dating from the 9th-10th century, is an excellent example of their work. Later Glamis became a centre for the conversion of the Picts to Christianity. St. Fergus, Patron Saint of Glamis, travelled across from Ireland in the early 8th century, establishing the church as he went, before choosing Glamis as his place of rest. He is said to have lived in a cave on the banks of the Glamis burn and made use of a nearby spring to baptise the early converts to Christianity.

It wasn't until the early 14th century that Glamis once again began playing a significant role in Scottish history. After the capture and destruction of the Castle of Forfar from the English, by Robert the Bruce, it was never rebuilt. Thus when the King and court were visiting the area, they all resided in a royal hunting lodge at Glamis. David, Bishop of St. Andrew's dedicated a church to St. Fergus on the site of the present church in 1242. In the 15th century Isabella Ogilvy, wife of the 1st Lord Glamis, built the Strathmore Aisle which adjoins the church. It was used as the Strathmore family burial vault until the death of the 12th Earl in 1865. The remainder of the church was taken down in 1790 to make way for the present church. The Graveyard also tells its story. The earliest tombstone dates from 1630 and they include those of masons, weavers, farmers, brewers, bakers, metal workers and many other trades, often represented pictorially. They include the grave of Margaret Bridie. She made Forfar Bridies (meat pasties) famous and Glamis has had little credit for her hard work and initiative !

The Angus Folk Museum

"Whenever throughout Scotland there rose towers of a castle there was found the humble houses of a hamlet or village built under the shadow of the great pile". To this rule Glamis was no exception. The retainers and dependents of the Lords of Glamis, those who owed feudal service and allegiance, formed the early village community. In 1491, James IV made Glamis a *"burgh of barony"* and allowed it the privilege of holding a public *"fayre"* annually on the feast day of St. Fergus (17th November). Hence Glamis became a country town of considerable importance.

St. Fergus Well

A plan dated 1773, shows the village much as it exists today except for the Kirkwynd Cottages built in 1793 and the recent development to the west of the Dundee-Kirriemuir road. Many of the current houses date from the late 18th century and early 19th century. The Manse dates from 1788 and the School from 1839. In the late 18th-19th century the main industry was the flax trade. A spinning mill was built in 1806, employing 66. In 1836 the population of the village was 2,050, in 1910 it was 1,159 and in 1993 t had reduced to 790.

The village of Glamis has great charm and is well worth a visit. Amongst many features of interest are the church and the Pictish carved stone. Close by is the ancient St. Fergus Well and an attractive walk along the river. A major attraction housed in the Kirkwynd Cottages, previously a row of farm workers retirement cottages, is the Angus Folk Museum run by The National Trust for Scotland. This Museum vividly illustrates the former way of life of the Angus villagers.

Glamis and the Bowes Lyon Family

*stones which have witnessed six
hundred years of Scotland's history*

The brass Glamis lion is based upon one of the family's heraldic supporters. It was a Golden Wedding present to the 13th Earl and Countess from their children and can be seen in the Dining Room

Lyon

Bowes

Sir John Lyon of Glamis (d.1382) = Princess Joanna dau. of King Robert II

Sir John Lyon of Glamis (d.1435)

Patrick, 1st Lord Glamis (d.1459)

Alexander, 2nd Lord Glamis (d.1486)   John, 3rd Lord Glamis (d.1497)

John, 4th Lord Glamis (d.1500)

George, 5th Lord Glamis (d. unm. 1505)   John, 6th Lord Glamis (d.1528)

John, 7th Lord Glamis (d.1559)

Line of Descent

John, 8th Lord Glamis (d.1578)

Patrick, 1st Earl of Kinghorne (1575 - 1615)

John, 2nd Earl of Kinghorne (1596 - 1646)

Patrick, 3rd Earl of Strathmore and Kinghorne (1643 - 1695)

John, 4th Earl of Strathmore (1663 - 1712)

| John, 5th Earl (*dsp* 1715) | Charles, 6th Earl (*dsp* 1728) | James, 7th Earl (*dsp* 1735) | Thomas, 8th Earl of Strathmore (1704 - 1753) |

John, 9th Earl of Strathmore (1737 - 1776)= Mary Bowes

John, 10th Earl (*dsp* 1820)   Thomas, 11th Earl of Strathmore (1773 - 1846)

Thomas, Lord Glamis

Thomas, 12th Earl (*dsp* 1865)   Claude, 13th Earl of Strathmore (1824 - 1904)

Claude, 14th Earl of Strathmore, K.G., K.T., G.C.V.O. (1855 - 1944)
= Nina Cecilia Cavendish Bentinck

| Patrick, 15th Earl of Strathmore (1884 - 1949) | Hon. Michael Bowes Lyon | 4 brothers and 3 sisters | Lady Elizabeth Bowes Lyon = HM King George VI |

| John, Master of Glamis (*k. in action* 1941) | Timothy Patrick 16th Earl (1918 - 1972) | Fergus, 17th Earl of Strathmore and Kinghorne (1928 - 1987) = Mary Pamela McCorquodale | HM Queen Elizabeth II | HRH The Princess Margaret |

| Michael Fergus, 18th Earl of Strathmore and Kinghorne (b. 1957) = Isobel Weatherall | Lady Elizabeth Bowes Lyon (b. 1959) = Antony Leeming | Lady Diana Bowes Lyon (b. 1966) = Christopher Godfrey-Faussett |

| Simon Patrick, Lord Glamis (b. 1986) | Hon. John Fergus Bowes Lyon (b. 1988) | Hon. George Norman Bowes Lyon (b. 1991) |

Family History

'*I must own*' wrote Sir Walter Scott when he stayed a night at Glamis '*that when I heard door after door shut, after my conductor had retired, I began to consider myself as too far from the living, and somewhat too near the dead*'. Scott's feelings were understandable – Glamis reeks of history and is peopled with phantoms, be they genuine echoes of past occurrences or the figments of imaginations held in thrall by the very stones which have witnessed nearly seven hundred years of Scotland's history.

As far back as the 8th century Glamis was a holy place. St. Fergus came over from Ireland to preach and is said to have lived and died here. A number of Celtic stones in the vicinity date from this period and St. Fergus's Well is close to the kirk. The present Earl of Strathmore bears the name of the saint.

From earliest known records Glamis belonged to the Scottish crown. It was not originally a fortress which is why it stands on low-lying ground in the midst of the lush Angus landscape. Its original purpose was a hunting lodge for the King of Scots who doubtless enjoyed many a good day out in the forests which must then have been hereabouts. Its position on boggy ground provided some defence.

Family crest

When the three witches approached Macbeth, hailing him as '*Thane of Cawdor and of Glamis*', Shakespeare was guilty of a solecism as neither Glamis nor Cawdor are known to have been thaneages in the 11th century. Glamis makes its first appearance as a thaneage in 1264, a thane being a lord holding his lands of the Crown subject to the Scots customs of landholding at that time. Thaneages were gradually phased out to be substituted by Norman-style baronies after the death of Alexander III. Thus Robert II changed Glamis from a thaneage to a feudal barony (not to be confused with the English peerage title) in 1376, when he granted it to **SIR JOHN LYON**

King Malcolm II was mortally wounded in battle on Hunter's Hill near Glamis in 1034. He was brought to the Castle and died there where a chamber is still named after him. He was succeeded by his elder daughter's son, Duncan I, who was slain near Elgin (probably in battle) by his first cousin Macbeth (the son of Malcolm's younger daughter) in 1040. Macbeth, in turn, met a sticky end and although Shakespeare makes a great drama out of it, these events were not uncommon in the turbulent Scotland of those days when Kings of Scots were frequently slain by their heirs.

We must now leap the centuries to the year 1372. In this year Robert II, the first Stewart King of Scots, granted to Sir John Lyon of Forteviot the thaneage of Glamis for services to the Crown. In 1376 Sir John married the King's daugher, Princess Joanna. Soon after the marriage the King made Sir John, Chamberlain of Scotland, then the most important office in the disposal of the Crown, and having raised the thaneage of Glamis into a feudal barony, granted it to his son-in-law, the reddendo being a red falcon to be presented to the King yearly on the Feast of Pentecost. Known as '*The White Lion*' perhaps because of his very fair hair and pale skin, Sir John's arms were a blue lion rampant possibly as a pun on his name and as a special mark of royal favour this was later enclosed in what is known in heraldry as a '*double tressure flory counter flory*' - a decorative surround similar to that borne on the present royal arms of Scotland and known in Scotland as an augmentation: '*a royal tressure*'.

The Royal Hunting Lodge as it may have appeared pre-1404

The origin of the Lyon family is uncertain. They have been ascribed the usual Norman descent by early genealogists, though it is more likely that they were of Celtic origin and a sept of Clan Lamont with a pedigree stretching back to the 4th century. As a cadet of the Lamonts, Sir John would have been armigerous anyway and the royal tressure merely a mark of favour granted by a King to his son-in-law.

The fact that Sir John was a man of rank and substance (Forteviot being one of the ancient Celtic thaneages) is evidenced by his being considered a worthy spouse for the Princess Joanna and capable of holding the important office of Chamberlain. This alone suggests a Celtic origin as a knowledge of Gaelic would have been necessary.

Whatever the truth, Sir John (knighted 1377) founded a line of feudal barons and later earls which still flourishes at Glamis and dwells within its red sandstone walls. He met a violent end at the hands of Sir James Lindsay of Crawford, Scotland's ambassador to England. It it said that he was undiplomatically murdered in his bed.

His son, **THE SECOND SIR JOHN LYON**, began building the Castle, as we know it today, *c*.1400. He built the east wing – now housing the Royal Apartments – after his marriage to the great-granddaughter of King Robert II. Access to the Castle at this time was probably by an external stair to the first floor.

'*a royal tressure*'

His son, **PATRICK LYON**, was created a peer of Parliament in 1445 as Lord Glamis after being released by the English who had held him hostage for King James I of Scots. He became a Privy Councillor and Master of the Household in 1450. He began to build the Great Tower c.1435 which was completed by his widow in 1484. It was not however linked to the east wing for a further hundred years. The Great Tower, built in the shape of an "L", was a tall building, typical of many similar castles then being built throughout Scotland - primitive by later standards but fairly impregnable to attack.

There would have been a cellar on the ground floor and an entrance hall on the next floor reached by outer stairs. The next floor contained the Great Hall where the lord and his family would live and dine. Surrounding the Castle was a fortified court.

Tragedy struck the family after the death of **JOHN, 6TH LORD GLAMIS** who had the misfortune to marry a Douglas. Misfortune, because King James V who had been dominated by his Douglas stepfather and manipulated by other members of the Clan, became obsessed in his hatred of all of the name of Douglas and carried on a ruthless vendetta against them. Poor Lady Campbell (as Lady Glamis had become after her husband's death), a woman of impeccable character, of singular beauty and popularity, did not escape this depraved monarch's ferocity. A trumped-up charge of witchcraft was brought against her and she was condemned to be burnt at the stake as a witch. After long imprisonment in a dark dungeon, she was almost blind. Luckily her husband was dead and did not have to suffer seeing her being burnt alive outside Edinburgh Castle. Even her young son was condemned to death and imprisoned only to be released after the King had died.

the Palace House c.1404
built by Sir John Lyon

22nd August 1562 - Mary Queen of Scots arrives in the Courtyard and next day dines in the Great Hall, now the Drawing Room

Not content with this grave atrocity, the King considered Glamis Castle as forfeit to the Crown, occupied it and held Court there from 1537 to 1542. Many existing royal decrees and charters are dated from the Castle during this period. These events suggest the Castle was a comfortable and desirable place at the time.

When the young **7TH LORD GLAMIS** was released after James V's death and restored to his property by Act of Parliament, he found that the royal usurpers had plundered the Castle of all its most valuable things - silver, bedding and furniture had all been taken away. A happier event took place years after when in 1562 the daughter of the cruel James V visited Glamis and showed great favour with the owner, perhaps as reparation for her father's wickedness. It was, of course, Mary Queen of Scots.

The Queen was on her way North to be present in person at the quelling of a rebellion against her by the Gordons under the Earl of Huntly. She was accompanied by her four Maries who made a new tapestry chair cover to while away the time. The English ambassador who was present wrote to Elizabeth I that in spite of '....*extreme Fowle and Colde weather, I never saw her merrier, never dismayed*'.

The **8TH LORD GLAMIS** was Chancellor of Scotland and Keeper of the Great Seal. By the end of the 16th century he was described by the English Ambassador as having *'the greatest revenue of any baron in Scotland'* and of being *'very wise and discreet'*. At about that time the household consisted of '...a principal servitor and maister stabular, 2 servitors, a musicianer, master cook and browster (for the bakehouse and brewhouse respectively) foremen, a maister porter and his servant, a grieve and an officer'. The lady of the house would be attended by '2 gentlewomen, a browdinstar (embroiderer), a lotrix (bedmaker) and two other female servants'. Like his forebear, Sir John Lyon, he met his death at the hands of followers of the Lindsay family, though this time it was by accident.

His son, the **9TH LORD GLAMIS**, also bore the Christian name of Patrick, so popular with his successors. He, too, became a Privy Councillor having succeeded to the title and property as an infant of three. When only eight years old and while travelling in France the young master of Glamis had his portrait painted by a follower of the painter François Clouet. On the reverse is a portrait of George Boswell, his secretary.

Patrick 9th Lord Glamis (afterwards 1st Earl of Kinghorne) succeeded to the title and property aged three. This portrait by a follower of François Clouet, shows him wearing a fashionable lace ruff collar and a jewelled hat.

On the reverse is this portrait of George Boswell his secretary, ever-ready with quill pen behind his ear!

The 9th Lord Glamis was created Earl of Kinghorne by James VI in 1606. His title probably relates to the grant, by Robert II to Sir John Lyon in 1381, of the burgh of Kinghorne, in Fife, with the manor place, lands, rents and forests belonging to the king. This higher rank of peerage in some way redressed the wrong done to the Lyon family by James V. Kinghorne became one of the King's Privy Councillors and accompanied his sovereign south when he succeeded as James I of England. It is at the English Court that he might have met Shakespeare. The new Earl continued the long process of evolving the architecture of the Castle to a semblance of what it is today by remodelling the tower and stair turret in 1600 -1606.

The 2nd Earl of Kinghorne
by George Jamesone

The **2ND EARL OF KINGHORNE**, it is said, '... *coming to his inheritance the wealthiest peer in Scotland, he left it the poorest'*. This was largely because of his friendship with James Graham, Marquis of Montrose, with whom he joined forces. Montrose was at first a fierce Covenanter (against Popery and episcopacy) but later became more of a Royalist. There came a point when Kinghorne's conscience forced him to part company from his old friend when the latter took up arms against the Covenanters, and to throw in his lot against him. He even helped finance the Covenanting army against Montrose and thus beggared himself in the process.

Thus when Patrick, **3RD EARL OF KINGHORNE**, came into his inheritance he found his estates burdened with debts amounting to £40,000 - an enormous sum in those days. He was advised that his estates were 'irrecoverable' but after 40 years hard work and determination he restored his inheritance to solvency. Patrick obtained a new charter to his patent of peerage in 1677 and was afterwards known as 'The Earl of Strathmore and Kinghorne' as have been his successors ever since.

The 3rd Earl kept a diary which he called his 'Book of Record', the manuscript of which is in the muniment room. His father died of plague when he was three and he was maltreated by his stepfather. On leaving St. Andrews at the age of 17 he went first to Castle Lyon (now Castle Huntly) where he found all the furnishings had been sold, possibly to pay his father's debts, and he even had to borrow a bed from the Minister of Longforgan. He came to Glamis with his wife in 1670 and lodged in rooms at the top of the great stair – the only part of the Castle glazed at that time.

It says much for this young man that he managed not only to pay off his debts by strict economies, but also was later able to rebuild and improve Glamis Castle to very much its appearance today. This can be seen by examining the distant view of the building in the huge family painting of Strathmore and his sons in the Drawing Room. He wrote in his diary *'Tho' it be an old house and consequentlie was the more difficult to reduce the place to any uniformitie yet I did covet extremely to order my building so that my frontispiece might have a resemblance on both syds, and my Great Hall haveing no following was also a great inducement to me for reering up that quarter upon the west syd wch now is, so haveing first founded it, I built my walls according to my draught....'* David Scott-Moncrieff thought that this entry suggested that the Earl was his own architect.

Lord Strathmore remodelled the Castle. He added the west wing in 1679 giving a false symmetry. He swept away the courtyard buildings, laid out the main avenue at 45 degrees to the Castle so that the large stair became the centre of the composition. In front he created a baroque setting of courts, sculptures and vistas. The interiors were equally rich. He built and decorated the Chapel (see page 17) and adapted the old Great Hall of the Castle, which had already been made elegant with plasterwork in 1621, into a fine Drawing Room which turned out to be his favourite part of the Castle and described in the diary as *'My Great Hall, which is a room that I ever loved'*. He also kept a *'private buffoon'* or jester and was the last nobleman to do so in Scotland. This jester's motley is still preserved in the Castle and can be seen in the Drawing Room and a small copy of it, worn by the Queen Mother's brother when a boy at a fancy dress party, can be seen in the Family Exhibition Room. The jester himself, it is recorded, was dismissed for proposing to a young daughter of the house!

The 3rd Earl of Strathmore and Kinghorne by Jacob de Wet 1683 (detail)

The **4TH EARL OF STRATHMORE** married Lady Elizabeth Stanhope, a daughter of the 2nd Earl of Chesterfield. He had seven sons, two of whom became Lord Glamis, both predeceasing their father and four other brothers who succeeded to the Earldom in turn, the 8th Earl and youngest son being the only one who had an heir.

It was during the time of the **5TH EARL** that the family's royalist sympathies came to the fore again when he joined the Jacobite cause and was killed at the Battle of Sheriffmuir in 1715. The following year the **6TH EARL** entertained the Old Pretender – James VIII and III – at Glamis together with an entourage of 88, for all of whom beds were provided. The 'Old Chevalier', as he was known, touched for the King's Evil in the Chapel. It was said that a true Sovereign could cure sufferers of this lymphatic disorder, common at the time, by touching them – faith healing we would call it today. It is said that all the sufferers who came to Glamis during the few days James stayed there were cured. This was a sure sign to Jacobites that he was the rightful King.

John 5th Earl   Charles 6th Earl

When the 'Old Chevalier' left the Castle, he absent-mindedly left his watch under the pillow. The maid who cleaned out the room after he had left, stole it. Many years later, that maid's great-great-great-granddaughter returned the watch to Glamis Castle. This, together with a sword which he presented to his host are shown in the Family Exhibition (see page 25).

(see page 25)

John 4th Earl
by Sir Godfrey Kneller

The **9TH EARL** was a Representative Peer for Scotland. Scottish peers did not have an automatic right to sit in the House of Lords, but had to be elected by their fellow peers to do so. Lord Strathmore married a great Durham heiress, Miss Mary Eleanor Bowes, the daughter of Sir George Bowes of Streatlam Castle and Gibside together with estates in Hertfordshire and elsewhere. The Bowes were a family of ancient and honourable descent, Sir Robert Bowes being Elizabeth I's Ambassador to Scotland from 1577 to 1583. The 9th Earl pulled down the west wing, added new kitchens and the Billiard Room in 1773 and new service courts beyond the east wing. He began remodelling the policies pulling down the garden walls in front of the Castle and moving, in 1775, the gates to the periphery of the policies.

The Castle as it appeared in 1775
watercolour by Thomas Girtin

The **10TH EARL** was also a Representative Peer, but was given the U.K. title of Lord Bowes which entitled him to a seat in the Lords without election. He took the name of Bowes and later the surname Lyon was reincorporated to form the present name of Bowes Lyon. He also quartered the arms of Bowes with his own. The former were also punning arms - three bows 'proper' on an ermine background, and so the family are a great rarity in having punning arms for both their surnames on the same shield. Although he lived largely on his estates in County Durham he completed much of the work at Glamis begun by his father. He re-roofed the east wing in 1797 and rebuilt the west wing 1798 -1801.

John 9th Earl
by Nathaniel
Dance

John

10th Earl of Strathmore

by Mather Brown

Thomas 11th Earl

The 10th Earl died in 1820 the day after his marriage and he was succeeded by his brother, the **11TH EARL**, when the barony of Bowes became extinct. The 10th Earl had a natural son by Mary Milner. He was John Bowes who founded the Bowes Museum at Barnard Castle. The Earl married Mary Milner in an unsuccessful attempt to legitimise John Bowes.

Thomas 12th Earl

Glamis Castle c. 1820 after the Baronialisation carried out by the 10th Earl of Strathmore

Claude 13th Earl

It was the **13TH EARL** who modernised and made the Castle into a comfortable home for his large family. Gas was introduced in 1865 to be replaced by electricity in 1929. He installed running water in 1865 and central heating in 1866. He built a five-acre walled garden in 1866 to provide vegetables, fruit and flowers for the Castle and in the same year re-opened the chapel. He refaced the servants courts beyond the east wing in 1891-97 and in 1893 created the Dutch garden in front of the Castle.

Saturday 23rd September 1883 - Queen Victoria's Prime Minister Mr. Gladstone is entertained in the Dining Room

The Dutch Garden laid out by the 13th Earl in 1893

The twentieth century brought further royal connections to Glamis with the marriage at Westminster Abbey on the 26th April 1923 between Prince Albert, Duke of York, second son of King George V, and the Lady Elizabeth Bowes Lyon, youngest daughter of the **14TH EARL OF STRATHMORE**.

This marriage was very popular in Scotland as it strengthened the very real ties of affection between the nation and the Royal Family which had been given such an impetus by Queen Victoria and Prince Albert. The Duke and Duchess not only shared a descent from Robert II, they were also both descended from King Henry VII, the Duchess through her mother, the Countess of Strathmore, who was a Cavendish Bentinck of the family of the Dukes of Portland.

Lady Elizabeth was the youngest of four daughters of the 14th Earl and his Countess. Lady Violet the eldest, died in childhood; Lady Mary married the 16th Lord Elphinstone and Lady Rose became the wife of Vice-Admiral the 4th Earl Granville.

Claude 14th Earl - father of HM Queen Elizabeth the Queen Mother by de Laszlo

The coat of arms of HM Queen Elizabeth the Queen Mother designed by Archbishop Bruno Heim, the former Papal Nuncio

Although Lady Elizabeth spent much of her childhood at Glamis she was not born here. Her younger daughter, Princess Margaret Rose, Her Royal Highness The Princess Margaret Countess of Snowdon, was born at Glamis in 1930 and was the first royal baby in direct line to the English throne to be born in Scotland for 300 years. This is proudly remembered at Glamis.

Commemorative panel displayed in the Restaurant celebrating the Coronation of King George VI with his Duchess as Queen Consort (ultimately HM Queen Elizabeth the Queen Mother)

At the Abdication of King Edward VIII the Duke of York ascended the Throne as George VI with the Duchess as Queen Consort and, ultimately, HM Queen Elizabeth the Queen Mother.

The eldest of the Queen Mother's six brothers succeeded as **15TH EARL**, served in the Great War in the Black Watch and married a daughter of the 10th Duke of Leeds. His elder son, John, Master of Glamis, was killed in action in the Second World War while serving in the Scots Guards and the 15th Earl was succeeded by his surviving son, Timothy, who also served in the Black Watch. The 16th Earl opened the Castle to visitors in 1950.

Patrick 15th Earl

The **16TH EARL** died in 1972 and was succeeded by his cousin Fergus Michael Claude, **17TH EARL OF STRATHMORE AND KINGHORNE**, son of Michael, 5th son of the 14th Earl. Educated like so many of his family at Eton, he went on to Sandhurst and became a Captain in the Scots Guards. He married Mary Pamela, the younger daughter of Brigadier N.D. McCorquodale and died in 1987. He is survived by his widow, Mary Countess of Strathmore and Kinghorne, their two daughters Lady Elizabeth Leeming and Lady Diana Godfrey-Faussett and was succeeded by their only son, MICHAEL 18TH EARL OF STRATHMORE AND KINGHORNE.

Timothy Patrick 16th Earl

Fergus 17th Earl

The present Lord Strathmore is married to Isobel, daughter of Captain A. Weatherall, and they have three sons: the heir Simon Patrick, Lord Glamis, the Hon. John Fergus Bowes Lyon and the Hon. George Norman Bowes Lyon.

Arms of the 18th Earl of Strathmore and Kinghorne

Michael Fergus 18th Earl of Strathmore and Kinghorne

The Earl and Countess of Strathmore and Kinghorne by the Castle's Dutch Garden with their children; the Hon. George Norman Bowes Lyon, Simon Patrick Lord Glamis and the Hon. John Fergus Bowes Lyon

HM Queen Elizabeth the Queen Mother with the Earl of Strathmore and Kinghorne in the grounds of Clarence House, after the State Opening of Parliament. Lord Strathmore is wearing the uniform of a Captain of the Yeoman of the Guard

So long as poetry, romance, religion, have a place in Scottish life and character, the Castle of dim memories, of secrets and haunting shadows, crowned with the beauty and dignity of years, will win men's hearts by a mysterious fascination, and stir them to their very depths.

The Rev. John Stirton

Glamis Castle
Glamis
Angus DD8 1RJ
Scotland
Telephone + 44 1307 840393 / 840242
Fax + 44 1307 840733
Email glamis@great-houses-scotland.co.uk
www.great-houses-scotland.co.uk/glamis